SAVE TREE SAVE LIFE

SAVE TREE SAVE LIFE

DR TAMANA BAHLOL

Copyright © Dr Tamana Bahlol
All Rights Reserved.

This book has been published with all efforts taken to make the material error-free after the consent of the author. However, the author and the publisher do not assume and hereby disclaim any liability to any party for any loss, damage, or disruption caused by errors or omissions, whether such errors or omissions result from negligence, accident, or any other cause.

While every effort has been made to avoid any mistake or omission, this publication is being sold on the condition and understanding that neither the author nor the publishers or printers would be liable in any manner to any person by reason of any mistake or omission in this publication or for any action taken or omitted to be taken or advice rendered or accepted on the basis of this work. For any defect in printing or binding the publishers will be liable only to replace the defective copy by another copy of this work then available.

- Acknowledgements Trees play an important role in maintaining our planet's ecosystem. Without trees, life on earth will not be able to survive. Trees are involved in many different aspects of life's survival. Food and oxygen are provided by trees, so we can live. Trees help our environment in many ways. Trees purify the air and give us oxygen for breathing. Without trees, we will lack fresh air which will lead to several life-taking diseases. Human knows very well that without trees our life would be a disastrous one but yet trees are cutting down for several purposes that are affecting nature in many ways. As a result of deforestation in the modern age, trees are no longer providing the beneficial benefits they once did.

Contents

CHAPTER ONE

• Trees form the most essential component of our environment. They take in sunlight, water and carbon dioxide to produce oxygen which helps support all forms of life on earth. Without trees, survival is impossible as there will be no food for animals or human beings. We simply cannot live without trees. Trees are like the lungs of the earth. They consume carbon dioxide and provide us with fresh oxygen to breathe. They keep clean air. Human beings and herbivores are largely dependent on them as they are sources of food. Coconuts, hazelnuts, apples, cherries and pears are just some of the delicious foods that come from trees. Trees make the mother earth look beautiful and relaxing. They nourish various life forms in many ways. Planting more trees will also add to the earth's natural beauty. Trees fight water pollution and prevent soil erosion. Tree roots hold the soil in hills or fields in place and prevent it from being blown away by water or wind. When trees are cut down, an area can quickly become a windswept desert. Fallen leaves from trees turn into mulch which makes the soil full of vital minerals and other nutrients for other plants and animals to thrive in. Trees prevent floods as their roots form a physical barrier to water runoff and stop the soil from being washed away. Further, the tree roots also suck water up from the soil and help to prevent flooding. They prevent pollutants from flowing into water sources. Humans are blessed by nature with many benefits. Our wellbeing and vitality are enhanced by being able to breathe clean air, drink clean water, and eat wholesome food. Nature freely provides us with these necessities. Some of the components of nature that make up the Earth's ecosystem include soil, atmosphere, sunlight, water, and living organisms. One of the living organisms that play a very crucial role in maintaining the Earth's ecosystem is trees. A tree is one of the most beautiful gifts of nature to mankind. Trees are also capable of absorbing a wide range of pollutants like Carbon monoxide and Sulfur dioxide. Trees (green mufflers) also absorb sound to reduce sound pollution. Insects, birds, and several animals find protection in trees. When trees are cut, these species would lose their shelter and their lives would be completely disrupted. Thus, life cannot exist without trees. Taking down trees for no good reason is something that should be eliminated. So, we can say that if we want to save our life, we must first save trees. Trees maintain the ecological balance of the environment. Trees form a natural habitat for animals, birds, insects, and wildlife. Noise pollution and air pollution are also controlled by trees. If we cut down more and more trees, pollution will increase and it will affect human life as well as of animals, birds, and fishes. Fine particulates present in the air are trapped by trees in their leaves and bark, making the air we breathe cleaner. Many industries like rubber, paper, medicine, etc., are dependent on trees and their products. Trees are our friends in need. They are the closest friends we have. Most of the thing that we need in our life comes from trees. We can't live without trees. In a way, trees are the lifeblood of the earth. Without them, we would not be able to live on Earth. The trees provide us with food, gum, and medicine. They provide us with oxygen for a healthy life. In addition to this, trees absorb carbon dioxide, which helps to reduce pollution. Timber produced by trees is used for many things including the construction of houses, train compartments, large boxes, tools, etc. The lack of paper may complicate our lives in some manner. Having a paper is essential for writing and studying. Firewood is used by villagers for cooking their meals. For purposes of building huts, houses, carts, and agricultural tools, people use wood as a building material. Trees are part of the natural beauty that surrounds us. A garden without flowers/trees wouldn't be as appealing as it is. The environment is thus improved by trees. Moreover, trees are responsible for rain, and they protect groundwater sources. This prevents droughts and floods, as well. Importance of the basic trees commercially Commercially, trees are used for a wide range of purposes. A wide variety of products can be derived from their wood, including paper, medicines, chemicals, and timber. A wide variety of food products are 8also extracted from trees including fruits, spices, and nuts. The bark of trees is rich in various substances, including cork, tannins, and cinnamon, as well as various dyes. Tree leaves are used to manufacture twine, rope, mats, etc. There are a variety of products that can be produced from the fluids in trees, including rubber, maple syrup, and turpentine. The importance of trees in humans' lives can be understood by the fact that trees are known as the "green gold" on Earth. It will not be possible to clean and refresh the polluted air without trees. People would then suffer from breathing problems, and/or respiratory disorders due to the polluted air. How we can save trees: (1) Plant a tree on a special date every month. Not only on Earth Day. (2) Use second-hand books instead of buying new books. It saves both money and paper, which automatically saves the trees. (3) Trees must be protected from fire and other manmade disasters. (4) Campaigns, processions and rallies can be organized to promote reforestation and tree planting. (5) Large number of people should gather for campaigns to request people to plant trees in their surroundings. In today's world different environment-related crisis like global warming, environmental pollution, melting of glaciers, etc., are common. These problems are the result of deforestation. Such problems can be controlled by planting more and more trees. From childhood, we have heard that trees are our best friend but in practical life, we didn't see anyone who treats trees as their friends. Although they are the most valuable life source on the earth. They benefit every life form in a direct or indirect way. And the earth is connected to them to maintain a natural We are discussing the reason why our friends need saving. They nourish us and protect us in many ways. Also, they keep our environment green and clean. So, it becomes our responsibility to repay them for the things they do for us by saving them. Besides, large trees are more beneficial than small ones because they capture more carbon, capture more water, combat the heat, filter greenhouse gases, gives shelter from heat and sunlight, etc. So, it can be said that we depend on them more rather than they on us. The human has become aware and serious about this issue and started doing the best they can do to save trees. The forest departments and government have banned the illegal cutting of trees. And they are going digital so that they can save paper which will reduce the number of trees cut down for making paper. Apart from that, the forest area after cutting of trees should be replanted with new ones. Also, we should teach our children to plant trees and ask them to pass it on their friends and acquaintances. The least that we can do is to plant some pots in our home rooftops or garden and ask our neighbor to do the same. Also, if we see the removal of a tree then we should inform the local authority about it to create awareness. Above all, strict laws should be made for people who illegally or without permission cut these trees for their own benefits. The various life form is able to survive on earth due to plants. If we remove plants from the earth even for one day then the survival of man will become difficult. Besides, they are the source of water and fresh oxygen on earth. Cutting trees means destroying life on earth. So, the time has come that we to be responsible for the action we have done till now. And start finding ways to save this Green Gold. 1) Trees are the heart of nature. 2) Trees help human beings in various ways. 3) Trees provide us with fresh air. 4) Trees provide us with food and shelter. 5) Trees are the home of several animals and birds. 6) Trees help reduce pollution. 7) We should save trees for the future. 8) We should plant more and more trees to promote healthy living. 9) Cutting trees without a good reason will affect our life. 10) If we will not save trees today, we will have to face several disasters in the future.

Every individual has a role to play in saving trees, and all of us need to contribute. We will only be able to achieve Saving Trees when each and every one of us take part in this great cause. In order to save the trees that are about to die due to a lack of water, we should water them as soon as possible. It is important to plant trees in all possible places in order to counterbalance the loss of trees caused by deforestation. Creating awareness among people is important so that they understand the importance of saving trees for the future. Generally, rural areas are more green and leafy due to the presence of trees so the people there live a very healthy lifestyle. People in cities do not have access to this greenery, so they are more susceptible to diseases and other problems. As a society, we all must stand today that we will not permit anyone to cut down trees and plants in the future. Furthermore, we will be planting trees every month in our locality. Plants, such as the ones planted by us today would be the life for the next generation. There is an eternal bond between human and trees. Trees help human beings and other living creatures in many ways. They supply oxygen to them. Trees give them food, fruits, fuel, timber, medicine, and many other useful things. They are also the harbingers of rain and check soil erosion. They give men shelter and shade. They protect the wildlife. Trees help men fight against environmental pollution. So we all must grow more trees and stop deforestation. We must save trees for our own sake. Human and trees have been in association with each other since the dawn of civilization. Trees provide man with timber for buildings and furniture, firewood, food like fruits, honey, goods of economic importance like rubber, resin, gums, and medicinal substances like turpentine, quinine, etc. Man is dependent on trees for his existence on earth. They produce oxygen (CO2) which keeps man alive. Trees also cause rainfall, prevent soil erosion and fertilize the soil. Of late, there have been massive schemes of deforestation afoot. Trees are felled recklessly. Forest areas are converted into human habitations. We must save trees for our own sake. To save civilization from extinction new programs of afforestation have been taken by the Governments. The festival, is observed every year in the rainy season. Thousands of saplings are planted on the occasion. More and more areas are brought under forest cover and people are taught "Plant trees and save a life." Trees are of great importance in our everyday life. They provide us with thatch for huts, timber for buildings and furniture, firewood, food like fruits, honey, etc., and medicine. We are dependent on trees for our very existence on earth. They produce oxygen which keeps us alive. They also absorb carbon-di-oxide exhaled by us and thereby help to create a pollution-free atmosphere. Trees help to prevent the erosion of soil and floods. Both the urban and rural people gain advantages from growing more trees. The former enjoys a pollution-free atmosphere and the latter get fruits, fuel, goods of economic importance, and medicines. Road-side trees are planted to beautify the roads and purify the air. Trees supply fresh air to reduce pollution in urban areas and help in rural economic growth. It is important to note that 33% of the land is required as forests in any country to maintain ecological balance. Trees help men fight against environmental pollution. We must save trees for our own sake. So we all must grow more trees and stop deforestation. We must care for trees for our own sake. Trees are considered an indispensable part of the environment. It is very necessary to save trees on this earth to make this earth safe for us. Trees are the most essential part of nature. It gives us life by providing oxygen to us. We all know the importance of trees in the environment. Thus it is said that 'save trees save the earth'. We can't survive on this earth without the presence of trees. So, the plantation of trees is very necessary to get a balanced environment for survival. We all know the importance of trees and thus we all should try to save trees. Trees are the best gift of nature to human beings. We can't ignore the importance of trees. Trees are very necessary for this planet to survive. That's why it is said that saving trees save a life. Trees serve as the best friend of human beings. Trees provide us with oxygen and absorb carbon dioxide from the environment. It also controls environmental pollution. Trees are the source of medicine and food for us. It also helps us in making our houses, furniture, etc. We need to plant more trees to enjoy the benefits of trees. It is said that saving trees saves the environment. We, human beings can't survive on this earth for a day without trees. Trees are the most essential part of the environment. It provides us with Oxygen to breathe in and absorbs CO_2 to maintain the balance in the environment. Human beings are completely dependent on trees for food, medicine, and many more. But unfortunately with the rapid growth in population deforestation is taking place. The number of trees is alarmingly decreasing in the environment. In order to live on this planet, we need to save trees. Not only human beings but all the other animals also depend on trees directly or indirectly to survive on the earth. So it is said that save trees and save animals. More plants should be planted to increase the number of plants. Awareness should be spread among people by organizing different competitions like save trees posters, save tree fancy dress competitions, etc. among students. We can't save the earth without trees so it can be concluded that save trees save earth. We all know the importance of trees. We should make people aware that trees are very important and also teach them why trees are important for us. Though there are 100 ways to save trees, people nowadays are not very conscious and don't want to save trees, so the government should take steps to save trees. People nowadays also after knowing how to save trees they are not trying to save trees. The answer to the question of how to save trees is very easy but people are not paying attention to it the simple answer to the question of how to save trees is, to stop cutting trees. Some of the things that would happen if people don't save trees are global warming, soil erosion, etc. people just talk about the benefits of trees but they are never seen trying any of the measures to save tree. People should not only talk about the importance of trees, but they should also try to implement the measures. Let's talk about things so that children also learn why trees are important to us. The first thing we should do is to teach the children how to save trees and why we should save trees. First, we should learn how to save trees. We can help by protecting the trees that grow in our own neighborhood, and planting more when you see trees cut down. Efficient use of paper products is important we can also help save trees by motivating others to plant more and more trees, what would happen if the trees decrease in number, and also by making them aware of the usefulness of trees. The following steps can be taken to save trees: Use paper in a wise manner; don't waste paper in a stupid way. Using secondhand books instead of buying new books it saves both money and paper which automatically saves the tree. (This is an important point we can teach everyone so that they learn how to save trees) Plant a tree on a special date every month. Not only on earth day. The forest fire is a high reason for numerous numbers of trees dying. We should be care full with fire, especially in forest areas where lots of woods are there both dead and living. We should never play with matches or lighters. We should always make sure that our site fire is completely out before leaving it. We should all know the importance of trees on the environment as trees clean the air. Tree works as a natural air sift of particulate matter such as dust, micro-sized metals, and pollutants such as oxides, ammonia ozone, nitrogen, and sulfur dioxides. Trees take in carbon dioxide and produce oxygen which is very important for every organism alive. Therefore, we all should plant more and more trees. By now everyone must be aware of how to save trees but also after knowing it people are not following the measures to save trees, in place they are just putting more and more trees for their personal needs. We know that the trees are responsible for cleaning most living creatures' breath. They give humans and animals materials to build their houses. Among many other uses trees give humans the materials that people use every day that's paper. A tree does all these for humans but in return what we humans are giving to the trees? We shameless humans are just killing trees one after another. So we should make every people aware of how to save trees and also try our best to know more from others too. We should all perform the task to save trees and tasks so that everyone knows it too. Many kinds of trees are endangered only because of us shitty people, endangered means the species which are close to extinction. And it's up to humanity to make the efforts needed to save wildlife from this tragedy. All this needs a simple gesture in the right direction, like focusing on special rights that protect trees. After knowing the importance of trees we should also perform tasks so that other peoples also know the benefits of trees. But only knowing how to save trees is not enough we should also try to save more and more trees and plant more and more trees. We all know that trees are the best friend of humans as trees provide us with every necessary thing from medicines to shelter. There are trees that provide us with very useful medicines to cure many diseases. Trees also provide us with edibles that can fill our tummy like fruits, veggies, etc. trees also provide us with oxygen which is the main requirement for the living of a living being. Without trees, life would be impossible on this planet earth. People nowadays even after knowing how to save trees they are not saving trees they are cutting more and more trees. Can we call this humanity? We can likely see that before trees humanity on this planet earth would endanger. This is a huge shame for every single human being living on this planet earth. We the educated people should first start to save trees and stop cutting trees and from we educated people, other people could learn why we should preserve trees, plant more and more trees and obviously stop the cutting of trees. If we human beings do so we can shamelessly say this earth to be an air pollution-free earth as the trees are responsible for cleaning the air. If more trees are there then there would be no polluted air, the air around would be clean and we could breathe clean air as much as we want to. So we should tell people about the importance of trees and also attempt our most excellent to save trees. Trees are the reward or simply the blessing of the so-called god to every living organism on this earth. There are different types of trees. Trees make landscapes stunning. Trees are valuable to man and terrestrial life forms. Trees maintain ecological balance and stability. Trees must be secluded. The felling of trees ought to be prohibited. Tree plantation activities should be encouraged to make our environment green, beautiful and healthy. Trees are food for human beings and every herbivorous animal. The roots, stems, leaves, flowers, fruits, and even the seeds of different trees can be eaten. Trees are Nature's bounty. We should not cut trees for our selfish needs. We should plant more and more trees and protect every single tree in or near our locality. To grow, a plant performs a process known as photosynthesis. In this process, plants absorb carbon dioxide and give out oxygen which we people breathe. The process carried out by plants also helps us in many other ways. Plants use up carbon dioxide and thus prevent the accumulation of greenhouse gas that leads to global warming and climate change. This is why tree plantation actions must be optimistic. There are many uses of the trees, some of them are: Trees provide shade. Trees combat climate change. Trees clean the air. Trees provide oxygen. Trees are even responsible for saving water. Trees help to prevent air pollution. Trees help prevent soil pollution. Trees provide shade. Trees provide food. Trees mark the season. Trees provide shelter for any living organism. Trees are also known as green gold. Trees are the children of our motherland, earth. Earth feeds the trees from its breast but we selfish people are killing the trees on a huge figure of deforestation is taking place in every outskirt of the city. People are killing trees for their selfish needs. These selfish people should be made aware of the absence of trees, and what would happen if trees would not have been there. Trees made life possible on this earth. The existence of trees made life possible on earth. We should not cut trees, planting more and more trees motivate others to plant a single sapling on their birthdays or maybe on a special day of theirs. Trees also reduce the amount of carbon dioxide in the air which is responsible for keeping the atmosphere around us not so hot. We should save trees. SAVE TREES SAVE LIFE. In today's world, different environment-related crises like global warming, environmental pollution, and melting of glaciers are very common. These problems are the result of deforestation. Such problems can be controlled by planting more and more trees. Thus it is said that save trees save life.

www.ingramcontent.com/pod-product-compliance
Lightning Source LLC
Chambersburg PA
CBHW020858160726
47993CB00004B/1718